IEA Health and Welfare Unit

Choice in Welfare Series No. 4

EQUALIZING PEOPLE

Equalizing People

Why Social Justice Threatens Liberty

David G. Green

London
IEA Health and Welfare Unit
1990

First published in 1990
by
The IEA Health and Welfare Unit
2 Lord North St
London SW1P 3LB

© The IEA Health and Welfare Unit 1990

ISBN 0-255 36262-5

Typeset by the IEA Health and Welfare Unit
Printed in Great Britain by
Goron Pro-Print Co. Ltd
Churchill Industrial Estate, Lancing, West Sussex

Contents

Acknowledgements

I have benefited greatly from the advice of Peter Collison, Rudolf Klein, Robert Pinker, Sir Reginald Murley, Arthur Seldon, Ralph Harris and other members of the Advisory Council of the IEA Health and Welfare Unit, not all of whom share the views expressed in *Equalizing People*. As always I must record my special thanks to Ralph Harris and Arthur Seldon for their efforts on my behalf and thanks are no less due to Caroline Quest and Marjorie Hutton for their comments on early drafts.

David Green

The Author

Dr David Green is currently the Director of the Health and Welfare Unit at the Institute of Economic Affairs. He was formerly a Labour councillor in Newcastle upon Tyne from 1976 until 1981, and from 1981 to 1983 was a Research Fellow at the Australian National University in Canberra.

He is the author of several articles on politics and social policy and his books include *Power and Party in an English City* (Allen & Unwin, 1980), *Mutual Aid or Welfare State* (Allen & Unwin, 1984) (with L. Cromwell), *Working Class Patients and the Medical Establishment* (Temple Smith/Gower, 1985), and *The New Right: The Counter Revolution in Political, Economic and Social Thought* (Wheatsheaf, 1987). His work has also been published in journals such as *The Journal of Social Policy, Political Quarterly, Philosophy of the Social Sciences* and *Policy and Politics*.

The IEA has published his *The Welfare State: For Rich or for Poor* (1982), *Which Doctor* (1985), *Challenge to the NHS* (1986), *Medicines in the Marketplace* (1987), *Everyone a Private Patient* (1988) and *Should Doctors Advertise?* (1989).

1

INTRODUCTION

After ten years of counter-revolution against the dominant collectivism of the post-war years, a new consensus is beginning to develop. Market competition is now widely accepted as the best way to create prosperity but market philosophy is still perceived by many as deficient. In particular, markets are said to foster selfishness. The remedy, according to socialist and social-democratic intellectuals, is to supplement market forces with 'social justice'.

Social justice and closely related concepts like 'positive freedom' and 'citizenship' all have an attractive ring. But in contemporary political usage they are synonyms for equality of outcome, the doctrine which demands that the power of the state should be used to equalize people. This paper is written in the belief that there are many of a socialist and social-democratic bent who have not yet appreciated the harm that will ensue if social justice, positive freedom and citizenship guide government policy.

In essence, each of these notions entails a call for the politicization of more aspects of each individual's life. Democracy, to the extent that it enables us to get rid of governments without bloodshed, is an unequivocal good but politicization of ever more areas of our private lives increases the power of the state at the expense of individuals, thus burdening politicians with multiplying distractions from their essential duties, and at the same time rendering each person less able to control his or her own affairs and more a pawn in a game played by whatever faction or fashion happens to control the government of the day.

There have been two main strands in British socialism embracing both production and consumption. On the one hand, British socialists shared the Marxist desire to put under government control the chief means of production, distribution and exchange; and on the other, they sought to achieve equality, or social justice, in consumption. There is now little desire for the nationalisation of the means of production and less desire for economic planning even among communists, because experience this century has taught that a market economy delivers prosperity whilst government control of prices and production obstructs it. However, the desire for 'redistributive justice' retains much of its old force. The new consensus among socialists accepts the market as the goose that lays the golden egg but the golden egg is to be distributed within the political system, not through the mutual adjustment of the market place.

The new socialism has, therefore, shifted its focus from *production* to *consumption*. It no longer desires to use the power of the state to take direct control of industrial production; instead it hopes to use state power to equalize consumption. The socialist desire for material equality, not only remains, but is being re-packaged and advocated with renewed vigour under the rallying cries of 'citizenship', 'social justice' and 'positive freedom'. It is also, however, tempered by the new realism. Few socialists aspire to bring about absolute equality; rather they believe there is a trade-off between equity and efficiency. Equality, therefore, is to be pursued only up to the point at which it is thought consistent with economic efficiency.

This idea strikes many as, at worst, harmless and at best thoroughly desirable and as a member of the Labour Party until 1981 I once shared this view. I can, therefore, understand its appeal but I now believe that experience of pursuing equality of outcome this century, not only in communist countries, shows that it is incompatible with a society of free individuals. Market competition should not be looked upon merely as a device for creating wealth which can then be parcelled out in the political process. It is inseparable from a wider vision of a society of thinking, valuing, choosing, and morally-responsible citizens.

From reactions to earlier drafts of this paper I know that this line of reasoning will anger those who see the pursuit of 'social justice' as a kind of middle way between the old statist socialism and unfettered capitalism. And there is a sense in which the pursuit of partial equality is preferable to absolute equalization, but the question remains: why use the power of the state to equalize incomes at all? There is a strong case for using the powers of government to prevent hardship, but once poverty has been eliminated why should the government concern itself in any way with the incomes people have? If there is a single overwhelming reason why supporters of social justice will be angered by my argument that equalization is incompatible with individual liberty, it is that socialism is seen as being on a higher moral plane than capitalism. I once took this view myself, but I now believe that to fail to see the centrality to capitalism of personal moral responsibility is to misunderstand its character on a grand scale. More than any other philosophy, capitalism (or classical liberalism) is based on a conception of the individual as a morally responsible agent.

Many intellectuals who identify with the left are making an effort to adjust to the reality that market competition creates prosperity and many have been willing to assert that the value of markets should be recognised by socialists. But they have not yet understood the moral character of capitalism. For decades capitalism has been characterised as callous and uncaring and socialism presented as humanitarian. The result is that it takes quite an effort for intellectuals to break with socialism because, at first, the choice seems to be as stark as that between good and evil. Having gone through this process myself I do not want to fall into the trap of being too harsh on those who are as yet still making the journey. And having been wrong once before, I hope the assertions I make in this paper are made with due reserve. But the fact is that the image of capitalism as an immoral system is a shallow caricature and the idea that socialism is morally superior is a monstrous exaggeration. Such thinking is the root cause of a number of intellectual blind spots which prevent many on the left from appreciating, not only that the pursuit of their own humanitarian objectives will be frustrated, but also the risk to civil liberty presented by policies of equalization.

Moreover, on closer inspection, the moral element of socialism turns out to be its demand for social justice. And social justice turns out to be the political demand that the power of the state be used to equalize individual incomes and possessions. Far from encouraging the altruistic side of human nature, the pursuit of equality promotes narrow selfishness by transforming the political process into a mechanism for profiting at the expense of other people.

The paper is organised as follows. Chapters 2 and 3 ask why social justice retains its attractiveness despite the harm that has already been done in its name, particularly since World War Two. An important factor has been the tendency to confuse the relief of hardship with redistributive justice. Relief of the hardship due to poverty has long enjoyed wide support, but I will suggest that it is very different in both its effects and its nature from equalizing or 'compressing' incomes. Support for the relief of hardship is based loosely on a sense that the rich ought to give out of their abundance to support the poor, but this is quite different from the desire to confiscate the possessions of others for purposes that go beyond the relief of hardship.

Most important of all is the claimed dislike of self-interest which is rooted in utopian socialist theories. I will examine how far modern theories of redistributive justice truly eschew self-interest and ask how far it can properly be said that markets encourage selfishness or acquisitiveness. Because the latter is the most powerful of the factors explaining support for social justice it is the subject of a separate chapter.

Chapters 4 and 5 examine the claim that renewed demands for equalization pose a threat to individual liberty, Chapter 4 focusing on the confusion between positive and negative freedom, and Chapter 5 on social justice and citizenship. Chapter 6 summarises the conclusions.

THE ALLURE OF 'SOCIAL JUSTICE':
Relief of Poverty and One Nation

The pursuit of 'social justice' is now enjoying a new lease of life as the focal point of Labour's appeal to the electorate but, notwithstanding its new realism, the Labour Party still shows insufficient awareness of the dangers of over-mighty government. In particular, the fatal confusion between freedom and power entailed in the distinction between positive and negative freedom is still fostered by the leaders of socialist thought, including politicians like Roy Hattersley and Bryan Gould and even academics like Professor Raymond Plant. The Social and Liberal Democrats are no less attracted to these ideas, as Paddy Ashdown's book reveals.[1]

Why does redistributive justice retain its appeal? Modern theories of redistribution have four main themes. First, there has long been a widely-supported belief that we all have a duty to relieve hardship. For most of British history the duty to help the poor was understood as a personal obligation, but now it is seen as one of the duties of the state. There is no automatic objection from a classical-liberal standpoint to the state undertaking this role, but the problem today is that the wide support for the relief of hardship has been exploited by egalitarians to cultivate support for equality, a doctrine calling for the power of the state to be used, not to assist the poor, but to equalize people.

Second, it is said that poverty should not exist alongside prosperity, from which it is inferred that the rich have a special obligation to help the poor. This notion is intermingled with two other sentiments: a sense of resentment towards the wealthy on the one

---

[1] Ashdown, A., *Citizens' Britain: A Radical Agenda for the 1990s*. London: Fourth Estate, 1989.

hand and, on the other, a desire to profit at the expense of other people. Third, providing for the poor is said to create social solidarity or 'one nation'. Political support for this idea is built partly on Bismarckian pragmatism aimed at deterring disorder among the lower orders and also on the Tory one-nation tradition rooted ultimately in a sense of common interest of the upper and lower classes reinforced by *noblesse oblige*. Among social policy analysts, however, the chief influence is citizenship theory. Fourth, equality draws its moral force from utopian theories condemning the pursuit of self-interest and advocating brotherly love. This chapter deals with the first three factors and Chapter 3 is devoted to the fourth.

Purloining the Welfare Impulse

The first foundation stone on which 'social justice' is built is the desire to relieve hardship. Among the achievements of egalitarians has been the concealment of policies designed to equalize people behind a smoke screen of compassionate talk about relieving poverty. This has enabled advocates of equalization to exploit support for the relief of poverty by falsely characterising measures designed to equalize people as measures to relieve suffering.

Defining Poverty

A particular landmark was the so-called rediscovery of poverty in the 1960s, when in reality poverty was not so much rediscovered as redefined. Instead of defining poverty in terms of hardship, the poverty line was calculated in relation to average earnings. Although the distinction came to be discussed as one between absolute and relative poverty, this mis-states the difference, because any definition of poverty based on hardship must be relative to the extent that public conceptions of hardship change over time. But the fact that conceptions of hardship have changed as prosperity has increased does not justify linking the poverty line to average or median earnings, with the result that a large proportion of the population is always said to be poor without regard to their actual standard of life. Some publications of the

Child Poverty Action Group (CPAG) exemplify the confusion at the heart of much analysis of this kind.

The Growing Divide, which assesses the first eight years of Thatcherism is typical.[1] In one of the essays, Professor David Piachaud reports that over the period from 1978 to 1987, the retail price index (excluding housing) increased by 86 per cent, the supplementary benefit (now income support) rate for a single person increased by 95.5 per cent and personal disposable income *per capita* increased by 122.5 per cent. Adjusted for inflation, recipients of supplementary benefit, therefore, enjoyed *increased* income in real terms of about 5 per cent, but the CPAG author prefers to focus on a comparison with average earnings and claims that supplementary benefit levels have *'fallen considerably'*.[2] He uses the term 'fallen' when in fact they have not fallen at all; they *increased* more slowly than average earnings. Indeed, on the same page he makes the very point that supplementary benefit levels have maintained and slightly increased their value in real terms under the Conservative government, but notes that they have not increased so rapidly as the incomes of others.[3] Yet, in his final assessment of the period 1978–1987 he disregards the distinction between 'falling' and 'increasing more slowly'.

Piachaud reports correctly that the number of people receiving supplementary benefit increased from 3 million to nearly 5 million, mainly due to unemployment. He then switches from talking about people *on* the supplementary benefit level to talking about those at or 40 per cent *above* it. Referring to persons in poverty or 'close to poverty' (that is, those with incomes up to 40 per cent *above* supplementary benefits), he reports an increase from 11,570,000 in 1979 to 16,380,000 in 1983.[4] This misleading use of language is the basis of the oft-repeated claim that one-third of the nation is poor. The facts are that 5 per cent of the population is *below* the

---

[1] Walker, A. and Walker, C. (eds.) *The Growing Divide: A Social Audit 1979-1987.* London: Child Poverty Action Group, 1987; cited hereafter as Walker and Walker (eds.), 1987.

[2] *Ibid.*, p. 22; emphasis added.

[3] *Loc. cit.*

[4] *Ibid.*, p. 25.

8

supplementary benefit level, about 11 per cent live *on* it and a further 19 per cent live on incomes up to 40 per cent *above* the supplementary benefit level. Yet Piachaud concludes that there has been a massive increase in the number 'left behind' and his final assessment is that the burden of poverty has 'increased grotesquely' during the first 8 years of Thatcherism.[1] In another essay, which uses the same evidence as Piachaud, Martin Loney of the Open University complains about the power of the media and blames it for enabling the government to *'reduce* the incomes of the poorest', when they have not been reduced in any sense.[2]

Professor Alan Walker in the same volume accuses the Government of trying to define poverty out of existence, claiming that 'time after time over the last eight years the Government has chosen to restrict the public's access to the truth about the social condition of Britain'.[3] He speaks of the increasingly divided nature of British society, particularly the 'fissure between rich and poor that has widened into a chasm since 1979'.[4] He also finds Britain grotesque:

> Economic "success" built on the foundations of grotesque inequalities, pauperisation and the illness and premature death of the poor in fact spells...economic and social disaster.[5]

Indeed, he finds Britain not only grotesque but uncivilised: *'By the weight of evidence and argument presented here, Britain in the mid-1980s is rapidly losing its claim to be a civilised society'.*[6] Martin Loney contributes a further use of the term 'grotesque'. The 'grotesque inequality' of contemporary Britain, he says, 'ultimately demeans us all.'[7] The frequent use of the term 'grotesque' suggests an aesthetic displeasure with the pattern of distribution but, in any

8

[1] *Ibid*, p. 26.

[2] Loney, M., 'A war on poverty or on the poor?', in Walker and Walker (eds.), 1987, p. 8.

[3] Walker, A., 'Introduction: a policy for two nations', in Walker and Walker (eds.), 1987, pp. 4-5.

[4] *Loc. cit.*

[5] *Ibid*, p. 7.

[6] *Ibid*, p. 6; emphasis in original.

[7] Loney, M., 'A war on poverty or on the poor?', in Walker and Walker (eds.), 1987, p. 18.

event, the assessment of these CPAG authors is unsupported by the evidence. In the period they studied, the standard of living of those on supplementary benefit increased in real terms. But this reality is masked by comparing supplementary benefit, not with the retail price index, but with average earnings and further masked by confounding people *at* or *below* the supplementary benefit level with people who earn up to 40 per cent *above* it.

Trickle Down

The same evidence used to confuse an increase with a decrease in the standard of living of the poor is also used in an attempt to rebut the argument of classical liberals that economic growth is the best way to raise the standard of life for all. It is often said that classical economists are indifferent towards the poor, if not downright callous, but a plain reading of the work of the classical economists from Adam Smith onwards reveals the contrary. Their constant pre-occupation was to understand how a nation could prosper in order that all its citizens could improve their standard of life, and their particular concern was to improve the conditions of the 'labouring classes'. Egalitarians call the process whereby the standard of life of all citizens is raised 'trickle down', a term which belittles it.[1]

Examination of the last 200 years plainly reveals that economic freedom has delivered greater prosperity for all. This is also the conclusion drawn by communist countries who are now openly abandoning socialism. The authors of *The Growing Divide*, however, chose to focus on the eight years from 1979–1987 and contend that evidence from that period proves that 'trickle down' does not work. Ignoring the long-run timescale applied by the classical economists and ignoring the plain fact that the standard of living of those on supplementary benefit increased in real terms between 1979 and 1987, Professor Alan Walker dismisses the Government's claim that a prosperous economy will benefit all citizens by pointing out that supplementary benefit rates did not

---

[1] For example, Lister, R., 'Conclusion II: There is an alternative', in Walker and Walker (eds.), 1987, p. 149.

increase as fast as average earnings between 1979 and 1987. The poor, he says, 'have got steadily poorer relative to the rest of the community over the last eight years, despite...economic growth'.[1] Professor Walker goes on to complain that the government has deliberately pursued policies of 'impoverishment and inequality'; and Martin Loney suggests in even more colourful language that 'the immiseration of a growing section of the population may be seen as an episode in the long standing struggle to maintain the status and privileges of the rich'.[2]

A more recent attempt to discredit classical-economic thought was made by the House of Commons select committee on social services. It reported an error in the Government's calculation of the earnings of low-income families between 1981 and 1985. Before the error (in the calculation of housing costs) was discovered it was believed that the incomes of the poorest 10 per cent of the population had risen by 8.4 per cent compared with the average of 4.8 per cent for the whole population, whereas the figure should have been 2.6 per cent compared with 5.4 per cent.[3] The conclusion drawn by many commentators was that trickle-down theory had been discredited.

But as I will argue more fully in Chapter 4, trickle down is the term commonly applied to the thinking of the classical economists who argued that the best way to overcome poverty is to understand the 'causes of the wealth of nations'. Adam Smith, for instance, was arguing against the old order, under which most people were born to a particular station in life and for whom material conditions hardly changed from one century to the next. For Smith, the solution to poverty was to set free human ingenuity by breaking the power of the guilds and the monopolists who prospered under the protection of one-sided laws.

Even if the incomes of the lowest ten per cent had fallen between 1981 and 1985, Smith's theory that free scope for human

---

[1] Walker, *op. cit.*, p. 3.

[2] Walker, A., 'Conclusion I: A divided Britain', Walker and Walker (eds), 1987, p. 129; Loney, M., *op. cit.*, p. 9.

[3] *Low Income Statistics*. House of Commons Social Services Committee, Fourth Report, 1989-90.

inventiveness, practical wisdom and initiative is the best way to end poverty would not have been disproved because the timescale he had in mind was longer. In any event, the incomes of the bottom 10 per cent increased.

Summary: Much discussion of poverty is marred not only by the use of exaggerated and emotive language but also by disregarding valid distinctions. It may or may not be a bad thing that supplementary benefit levels rose less rapidly than average earnings, but either way 'falling' remains distinct from 'rising'. No less important, there is a difference between being *at* or *below* the supplementary benefit level and being up to 40 per cent *above* it. Nor do the contributors to *The Growing Divide* make the least effort to justify linking the poverty line to average earnings. The average reflects a huge multiplicity of individual circumstances, including the success or failure of companies in meeting the demand for goods and services, labour mobility, personal choices between work and leisure, preferences for training and re-training, competition from foreign companies and so on. The public policy issue should not be whether the poverty line matches changes in an arbitrary statistical artefact like average earnings; rather it should be how to agree upon the acceptable minimum standard of life for a citizen of this country. The government's proper role is to prevent people falling below the minimum and to do so in such a way as to assist able-bodied recipients of benefit to become independent, self-supporting citizens as quickly as possible. Egalitarian partisans have also failed to see how equalization undermines the process whereby differential success in serving one's fellow citizens is signalled. But I will return to this issue in Chapter 4.

Profiting at the Expense of Others

It is often said that socialist policies of confiscation are based on envy. This has some truth in it but envy does not satisfactorily account for egalitarianism. The chief factors are twofold (a) the characterisation of the spending of the wealthy as frivolous and, therefore, unjustified whilst others suffer real hardship, and (b) the exploitation of the human desire to obtain something for nothing, when in reality the benefits are at the general expense.

If you said to any cross-section of the population that the wealthy few must give up their yachts so that the Income Support level can be raised there would be much agreement, at least at first, because spending on yachts is seen as frivolous. The problem is that the total amount of money spent frivolously is small and the end result of redistribution over the last 40 years or so has been the heavy imposition of taxes on people who are far from wealthy and will never be in a position to buy a yacht. Far from ending bad or wasteful patterns of life to help the poor, redistribution has meant eroding the income of the low-paid worker.

In any event, much personal spending is not frivolous, and reducing disposable incomes has meant that individuals and families are unable to accumulate savings sufficient, for instance, to invest in capital goods. There is a hidden assumption that the weekly wage represents the cost of physical support plus 'pocket money' for luxuries and conveniences from which it follows that there is no harm in the government taking part of it away. But the result has been insufficient investment in capital and, in the view of some, insufficient spending on cultural activities. A further unintended consequence has been that governments have taken responsibility for investment and cultural spending. Grant-making agencies like the Arts Council have been founded to encourage the arts, leading to still higher taxation and still further central power. And industrial investment has been encouraged, even under Mrs Thatcher, by direct subsidies from the taxpayer and by offering inducements to corporations to invest when similar incentives are not available to individuals or families. Thus, the perverse result of socialist policies of high taxation has been the enhancement of the power, not only of the state, but also of corporations at the expense of individuals and families. The consequence has therefore been redistribution, not from the rich to the poor, but from families to corporations and from all individuals to the state.

So far I have accepted that much support for redistributive justice is based on the widespread public desire to relieve hardship, but in reality it is also based on a rather lower motive. In practice much support for redistribution feeds on and stimulates selfishness by telling voters that they will benefit from taxes imposed on others. Professor Ruth Lister, for instance, a former director of CPAG, urges improvements in child benefit, pensions, the position of the long-term unemployed and the introduction of a phased disability income scheme, all of which she believes should be financed by taxes on the top five per cent of earners.[1] In doing so she is encouraging people to demand benefits at the expense of the wealthy when the reality of the welfare state for the majority is that they are being bribed with their own money.

The real significance of such bribery is that it has broken the traditional solidarity of all taxpayers against the over-spending proclivities of government. In Britain our liberties were built on this solidarity as monarchs from the Saxons to the Stuarts and their successors conceded individual rights and constitutional checks in return for taxes. The policy of governments this century has been to divide and rule by telling one section of the population that their benefits are at the expense of others. The result has been a higher burden of taxation than ever, and a particularly high burden on the low paid.

Selfishness is deeply ingrained in people. Children have to be taught the value of sharing and showing consideration to others but whatever our upbringing, selfish drives remain with us and for this reason it is important that our institutions discourage rather than promote narrow selfishness. Encouraging people to believe that they can benefit at the public expense achieves the very reverse. It fosters and breeds selfishness.

Social Solidarity

The third idea lending support to the pursuit of social justice is that of social solidarity, a principle to which the Thatcher Government is thought to feel little adherence. Indeed, it has been accused of deliberately creating two nations.

---

[1] Lister, R., 'Conclusion II: There is an alternative', in Walker and Walker (eds.), 1987, p. 148.

The desire for social solidarity has historically had various roots, including patriotism, nationality, race, religion, tradition and hierarchy. Even today, the Bismarckian desire to deter the 'lower orders' from rebellion and the Old Tory concept of social hierarchy retain some vitality. But the chief factor affecting social policy is the view that universal benefits avoid stigmatising the poor and create a sense of citizenship. For writers such as Richard Titmuss, the welfare state ought not to be seen as public charity. Instead it is the means by which people are integrated into the community and compensated if they are the victims of economic change.

Those who wish to integrate people through universal benefits believe that their policy will permit every person to become a citizen. This citizenship theory owes much to T.H. Marshall, who contended that before the welfare state people acquired political and civil rights to which we have now added 'social' rights, including welfare rights and social services. Social rights gave people the right to 'share to the full in the social heritage and to live the life of a civilized being according to the standards prevailing in the society'.[1] More recent advocates of citizenship theory claim that people are excluded from society if they are denied certain consumption opportunities and contend that this gives them a claim on the public purse.[2]

I will return to citizenship theory in Chapter 5 and for the moment must confine myself to noting that citizenship theorists fail to acknowledge that social solidarity is possible without equality of outcome. People may also feel a bond of loyalty towards institutions which offer a *minimum* without equality. And more important still, people may feel loyalty towards institutions because they provide opportunities for self development and for making private and unpoliticized contributions to the well-being of others.

---

[1] Marshall, T.H., 'Citizenship and social class', in T.H. Marshall, *Sociology at the Crossroads and Other Essays*. London: Heinemann, 1963, p. 74.

[2] Harris, D., *Justifying State Welfare: The New Right versus the Old Left*. Oxford: Blackwell, 1987, p. 148.

3

THE ALLURE
OF SOCIAL JUSTICE:
Brotherly Love and Acquisitiveness

The fourth source of support for social justice comes from utopian theories which have urged that by abolishing private property altogether we could end social antagonism and encourage more fraternal social relationships. In the Marxist tradition the abolition of private property was expected to bring about the withering away of the state. Now socialists accept private property, not only because in those countries which have abolished it antagonism has not diminished, but also because private property and market production have proved better able to bring about economic prosperity.

However, economic growth has not always been sought by socialists. Part of the allure of socialism has been the idea of sharing produce rather than competing for it. This much inspired the early Fabians like Sidney Webb, who found in socialism a substitute faith for his lost religious belief.[1] But sharing has worked only where possessions are not simply shared but also spurned altogether as, for instance, in a monastery. Most socialists, however, do not reject possessions totally. Socialism therefore:

seeks to restore...unity without the faith which causes it. It seeks to restore sharing as amongst brothers without contempt for worldly goods, without recognition of their worthlessness. It does not accept the view that consumption is a trivial thing, to be kept down to the minimum.[2]

---

[1] Webb, B., *My Apprenticeship*. London: Longmans, 1926, p. 143.

[2] De Jouvenel, B., *The Ethics of Redistribution*. Cambridge: Cambridge University Press, 1951, p. 12.

These words of Bertrand de Jouvenel have lost none of their relevance in the 40 years since they were first spoken. Earlier socialists like Tawney did eschew material goods beyond a certain level of consumption. No person, Tawney thought, should desire more material goods than those necessary to enable the individual to be of service to others, but his attitude has few adherents in today's Labour Party.[1] The Green Party, which opposes economic growth on environmental grounds, comes closer to Tawney's ideal.

Although the total rejection of material things has few supporters today, the moral appeal of socialism is still based on its claim to repudiate the relentless pursuit of self-interest. Modern socialist rhetoric often takes this line and many journalists have imbibed these assumptions, perhaps without much thought. Such talk is so pervasive it even appears in normally more reflective organs like the *Financial Times*. Michael Prowse, for instance, a leader writer and columnist on the *Financial Times* says this about Thatcherism:

> Those who care deeply about social justice have often felt themselves to be conducting a dialogue with the deaf... Society, in the eyes of Thatcherism, is an illusion: all that really exists are isolated individuals. The goal of policy should be to encourage maximum self-reliance and to give individuals maximum freedom to exercise their God-given preferences in the market place. ...the principle *raison d'etre* is the accumulation of material goods which are to be passed on to the next generation.[2]

Alongside the condemnation of self-interest, however, socialists also advocate faster economic growth, that is, the accumulation of material goods. And as de Jouvenel has written: 'If "more goods" are the goal to which society's efforts are to be addressed, why should "more goods" be a disreputable objective for the individual?'[3]

---

[1] Dennis, N. and Halsey, A.H., *English Ethical Socialism: Thomas More to R.H. Tawney.* Oxford: Clarendon Press, 1988.

[2] Michael Prowse, 'The isolation of the individual', *Financial Times*, 4 May 1989.

[3] De Jouvenel, *op. cit.*, p. 12.

People As Consumers

Now at the forefront of socialist thought is the idea of economic growth combined with equality of consumption. The idea of equalizing consumption rests on the view that consumer satisfaction is legitimate, but that access to the good things of life is unequal and should be made more equal. Consumer satisfaction as such is not challenged. Few socialists have understood precisely how shallow an ideal equality of consumption is. People are seen primarily as consumers or satisfaction seekers. No less important, the desire to equalise consumption ignores services which are not priced. This diverts attention away from services which are not commercialised such as the mutual services of husband and wife in marriage, the training and care of children within the family, voluntary help given to neighbours and friends or organised work for voluntary organisations. Indeed, much of what makes for a good and fulfilled life is voluntary and unrewarded. Advocates of equalization also neglect the extent to which individual incomes are often spent for the benefit of others: to give satisfaction to friends and neighbours, or to sustain what some might consider to be higher forms of civilisation. Moreover, the desire for equalization has promoted the tendency for the total worth of individuals to be reckoned in terms of the services for which they are remunerated.

Redistributionists think overwhelmingly in terms of consumer satisfaction, and their focus on equating satisfactions distracts them from the reality that there is more to life than consumer satisfaction:

> To the social philosopher interested in human beings it must seem absurd that one should be passionately interested in equalizing among these lives supplies of the "stuff", on the ground that absorbing the stuff is the stuff of life.[1]

---

[1] *Ibid.,* p. 53.

18

Socialism has enjoyed much support because it has been seen as based on the idealism of hoping for a better world with less antagonism and more caring relationships. But where is the idealism in the modern socialist vision of economic growth combined with the equalization of consumption? The reality is that modern theories of redistributive justice take much of their inspiration from the narrowest kind of selfish materialism. 'Social justice', in the sense of equal consumer satisfaction, hardly deserves to be classified as an ideal at all. De Jouvenel again:

> Nothing quite so trivial has ever been made into a social ideal... What is to be held against them is not that they are utopian, it is that they completely fail to be so; ...not that they wish to transform society beyond the realm of possibility, but that they have renounced any essential transformation; not that their means are unrealistic, but that their ends are flat-footed.[1]

Markets and the Encouragement of Acquisitiveness

Socialist writers in recent decades have been successful, not only in creating the impression that socialists are well intentioned, but also that anyone who opposes them is selfish. Even scholars like Professor Raymond Plant, who are making an honest effort to come to terms with the failure of socialism, still retain their doubts about markets. Writing jointly with an American colleague, Kenneth Hoover, Plant argues that the market encourages egoism over altruism:

> There may well be a place for markets in a humane society but they must be kept in their place, because they encourage some forms of behaviour rather than others, viz. egoism over altruism, and rational calculation of advantage over trust.[2]

---

[1] *Ibid.*, p. 48.

[2] Hoover, K. and Plant, R., *Conservative Capitalism in Britain and the United States: A Critical Appraisal.* London: Routledge, 1989, p. 232.

They claim that under what they call 'individualist conservatism':

What matters is the result of a person's endeavours and whether others are prepared to pay for it. This is the *only* criterion of value applicable in a free society.[1]

Professor Plant's doubts are those of a scholar who is trying to come to terms with the new realities, but it is difficult to detect scholarly caution in all leftist claims about the selfishness of capitalism. Professor Alan Walker, in the CPAG book cited earlier, for instance, denounces Thatcherism as 'the politics of selfishness' and argues that the British people will support an alternative strategy built on collectivist and altruistic values. Despite the 'constant barrage of exhortations for self-reliance and self-interest', these collective impulses, he says, 'keep reasserting themselves in the public opinion polls'.[2] In the same publication, Martin Loney of the Open University uses even stronger language. Greed, he says, has been elevated into 'a national religion'.[3]

This parody of classical liberalism as inhumane or greedy is widespread in social policy literature. In a typical recent contribution, *British Welfare Policy: Workhouse to Workfare*, Anne Digby, a lecturer at Oxford Polytechnic, interprets differences of view over social policy as a struggle between humanity and efficiency:

Setting the requirements of humanity in social welfare policies against those of efficiency in the market involves striking a balance between social and economic markets in our mixed economy. That the scales are tipping decisively against humanity is indicated by recent discussion of the desirability of workfare polices by politicians on the political right.[4]

---

[1] *Ibid.*, p. 51; emphasis added.

[2] Walker, A., 'Introduction: a policy for two nations' in Walker and Walker (eds.), 1987, p. 7.

[3] Loney, M., 'A war on poverty or on the poor?', in Walker and Walker (eds.), 1987, p. 19.

[4] Digby, A., *British Welfare Policy: Workhouse to Workfare*. London: Faber and Faber, 1989, p. 131.

In her summary, Digby says that a period of financial constraint appears to have made many voters 'more conscious of their purse-strings than their heart-strings'.[1]

Self-interest and Selfishness

The propaganda victory of the left in associating markets with selfishness is based largely on the confusion of self-interest with selfishness. But all instances of self-interest are not examples of selfishness. Self-regard may be selfish; equally it may not. We can understand this question better if we contemplate the extreme form of other-regarding, or altruistic, behaviour. The extreme form rejects all regard to self whatsoever, believing that even to make an effort to feed oneself diverts attention away from service of others or service of God. Mendicant Buddhist monks live according to such principles, refraining from work and relying entirely on begging for support. But we cannot all be beggars and it is therefore essential to human survival that most of us take the trouble to support ourselves and our dependents. Not to be self-interested in your own survival would be to impose on others and to that extent a failing; and self-support cannot be anything other than a matter of self-interest.

In seeking to support ourselves we therefore pursue our self-interest and since we live in a prosperous society it is legitimate for us to increase our own comforts as well as merely to provide for necessities. However, we may go about making efforts to support ourselves in a selfish or unselfish manner. And here lies the source of the confusion. Selfishness means consistently putting your own interests *above* those of others or consistently disregarding the interests of others. Self-interest means, at the minimum, providing for yourself instead of relying on others, but to the classical economists it primarily meant seeking to better your own conditions and those of your family. It was essentially a permissive doctrine, claiming only that there is no shame in seeking a better life through work, saving and trade. Whether an individual chooses

---

[1] Digby, *op. cit.*, p. 3.

only to earn sufficient income for self-support and no more, or whether he prefers to exert himself to rise above mere self-sufficiency is a matter of personal preference. But self-interest does not necessarily entail selfishness. A person can be self-interested and by a process of mutual adjustment to others avoid selfishness.

Adam Smith is well known for his claim in *The Wealth of Nations* that we need constant help from one another and that it is more likely to flow from self-love than benevolence. This observation has been the source of much misunderstanding, primarily because it is only part of what Smith has to say on the subject. To understand Smith's thinking it will help to know something of where his best-known book, *The Wealth of Nations*, fits into his wider work. His lecture course at the University of Glasgow, where he was professor of moral philosophy, was divided into four parts: natural theology, ethics, justice (or jurisprudence) and expediency. The fourth part, on expediency, formed the basis of *The Wealth of Nations*. The third section on justice was intended to be a book but remains available only as *Lectures on Jurisprudence*. The second section on ethics was the basis for *The Theory of Moral Sentiments*, which was also influenced by his lectures on religion. *The Wealth of Nations*, therefore, is far from containing all that Smith had to say. To appreciate Smith's contribution it is vital to understand what he has to say in *The Theory of Moral Sentiments* and because Smith's actual views are so different from the caricature often presented today, I will quote extensively from its pages.

Adam Smith on Morality

It may be unlovely that self-interest motivates people but it is a fact nonetheless. This observation, however, does not reflect cynicism, nor merely realism, on Smith's part. He believed, not only that it was perfectly proper for people to pursue their self-interest, but also pointed out that regard for others must always be built on self-interest because we have no other way of judging how others feel. The first precept of Christianity is:

22

to love the Lord our God with all our heart, with all our soul, and
with all our strength, so it is the second to love our neighbour as we
love ourselves; and we love ourselves surely for our own sakes, and
not merely because we are commanded to.[1]

We can only love our neighbours by putting ourselves in their
shoes, a process which Smith called 'sympathy', but which today
might be called empathy. It is the process by which we *imagine*
how we would feel if we were in another person's predicament
when, for instance, they look sad or happy or in pain or have just
received bad news.

Smith took pains to distinguish between his notion of sympathy
and selfishness:

> Sympathy, however, cannot, in any sense, be regarded as a selfish
> principle. When I sympathise with your sorrow or your indignation,
> it may be pretended, indeed, that my emotion is founded in self-love,
> because it arises from bringing your case home to myself, from
> putting myself in your situation, and thence conceiving what I should
> feel in the like circumstances.

But this does not make it selfish because when a person sym-
pathises with another he changes characters: 'My grief, therefore,
is entirely upon your account, and not in the least upon my own.
It is not, therefore, in the least selfish.'[2]

But self-love, Smith urged, should not be left to its own devices.
It should be tempered by conscience, or in one of his favourite
phrases, the 'impartial spectator':

> ...the natural preference which every man has for his own happiness
> above that of other people, is what no impartial spectator can go
> ·along with. Every man is, no doubt, by nature, first and principally
> recommended to his own care; and as he is fitter to take care of

[1] Smith, A., *The Theory of Moral Sentiments*. Indianapolis: Liberty Classics, 1969, pp. 283-84.
[2] *Ibid.*, p. 502.

himself, than of any other person it is fit and right that it should be so...

But, he insisted, we must view ourselves:

not so much according to that light in which we may naturally appear to ourselves, as according to that in which we naturally appear to others... If he would act so as that the impartial spectator may enter into the principles of his conduct...he must...humble the arrogance of his self-love, and bring it down to something which other men can go along with.[1]

Benevolence, Wisdom and Virtue

Thus, we must judge ourselves not by our own selfish inclinations but according to how others see us. But not just by how *any* other person sees us: the judge is characterised by Smith as the impartial spectator.

So Smith was not in the least cynical or ambiguous about selfishness. He regarded selfishness as a vice and benevolence as a virtue:

to feel much for others, and little for ourselves, that to restrain our selfish, and to indulge our benevolent, affections, constitutes the perfection of human nature; and can alone produce among mankind that harmony of sentiments and passions in which consists their whole grace and propriety.[2]

Nor did he display any particular admiration for the pursuit of wealth. Far from it:

This disposition to admire, and almost to worship, the rich and the powerful, and to despise, or, at least, to neglect, persons of poor and

---

1 *Ibid.*, pp. 161-62.

2 *Ibid.*, pp. 71-72.

mean condition...is...the great and most universal cause of the corruption of our moral sentiments.[1]

People, he thought, were much influenced by the respect and admiration of others. To deserve and to enjoy, the respect and admiration of mankind, 'are the great objects of ambition and emulation', but two methods were available to us: 'one, by the study of wisdom and the practice of virtue; the other, by the acquisition of wealth and greatness'.[2] He much regretted that:

> upon coming into the world, we soon find that wisdom and virtues are by no means the sole objects of respect; nor vice and folly, of contempt. We frequently see the respectful attentions of the world more strongly directed towards the rich and the great, than toward the wise and virtuous. We see frequently the vices and follies of the powerful much less despised than the poverty and weakness of the innocent.[3]

The Importance of Society

Collectivists also claim that classical liberalism is based on atomistic individualism. But Adam Smith took the entirely opposite view. Man 'can subsist only in society', he says, and much of his work was an attempt to understand the bonds which hold a society together in a complex economy which increasingly depended on the international division of labour. When Smith was writing, in the second half of the eighteenth century, life for many people had already ceased to consist largely of face-to-face relationships with close friends or associates and was more and more based on impersonal trading relations with strangers, including distant suppliers, customers and investors. This change from face-to-face to anonymous relations has been a recurring theme in Western political and sociological thought and Smith's insights into how a

---

[1] *Ibid.*, p. 126.

[2] *Ibid.*, pp. 126-27.

[3] *Ibid.*, p. 126

25

'great society' of people not intimately known to each other could be held together are as valid today as they were 200 years ago.

Society, he thought, could be held together according to three main principles: prudence (utility), beneficence (benevolence) and justice:

> Concern for our own happiness recommends to us the virtue of prudence; concern for that of other people, the virtues of justice and beneficence—of which the one restrains us from hurting, the other prompts us to promote that happiness.

Prudence, which he also calls utility, refers to the mutual advantage of exchange at agreed prices. Smith, however, did not believe that prudence was the last word on the subject. He believed that a society would be less happy and agreeable if it was held together by utility alone:

> Society may subsist among different men, as among merchants, from a sense of its utility, without any mutual love or affection; and though no man in it should owe any obligation, or be bound in gratitude to any other, it may still be upheld by a mercenary exchange of good offices according to an agreed valuation.[1]

But he thought it would be a much better world if it was based on benevolence and he certainly felt strongly that society 'cannot subsist among those who are at all times ready to hurt and injure one another'. But beneficence, he felt, was 'the ornament which embellishes, not the foundation which supports the building'. Justice was the vital element, or in his own words, 'the main pillar that upholds the whole edifice'. Beneficence, he thought was

> less essential to the existence of society than justice. Society may subsist, though not in the most comfortable state, without beneficence; but the prevalence of injustice must utterly destroy it.[2]

---

[1] *Ibid.*, p. 166.

[2] *Ibid.*, p. 167.

26

The distinction between justice and benevolence is that infringements of justice do positive harm and are rightly punished by the state, whereas the absence of benevolence does no actual harm, although human relationships are much the worse without it. Beneficence, said Smith, 'cannot be extorted by force, the mere want of it exposes to no punishment; because the mere want of beneficence tends to do no real positive evil'.[1] Justice is different and infringements may be punished:

> the violation of justice is injury: it does real and positive hurt to some particular persons, from motives which are naturally disapproved of. It is, therefore, the proper object of...punishment.[2]

The want of beneficence merits no punishment, but when practised it deserves reward in the form of praise. The practice of justice merits no praise, but want of it merits punishment.[3] (I will return to benevolence and justice in Chapter 4.)

There is no shadow of doubt or reluctance in Smith about the role of government—no ultimate desire to be rid of it altogether. Justice was the vital ingredient in any social order, and justice was the responsibility of government.

Vanity

Nor did Smith favour a narrow materialistic social order. Perhaps surprising to the modern reader, Smith reserves his harshest judgement for those who try to explain all human conduct in terms of self-interest:

> Some splenetic philosophers, in judging of human nature, have done as peevish individuals are apt to do in judging of the conduct of one another, and have imputed to the love of praise, or to what they call

---

[1] *Ibid.*, p. 155.
[2] *Ibid.*, p. 157.
[3] *Ibid.*, p. 159.

vanity, every action which ought to be ascribed to that of praisewor-
thiness.[1]

He singles out Bernard Mandeville for criticism:

Dr Mandeville considers whatever is done from a sense of propriety,
from a regard to what is commendable and praiseworthy, as being
done from a love of praise and commendation, or, as he calls it,
from vanity. Man, he observes, is naturally much more interested in
his own happiness than in that of others, and it is impossible that,
in his heart, he can ever really prefer their prosperity to his own.[2]

According to Smith 'the desire of doing what is honourable and
noble, of rendering ourselves the proper objects of esteem and
approbation' cannot properly be called vanity:

Even the love of well-grounded fame and reputation, the desire of
acquiring esteem by what is really estimable, does not deserve that
name.

It is, says Smith, 'a love of virtue, the noblest and the best passion
of human nature'. To be vain is to seek praise for qualities or
actions that are not praiseworthy.[3] The wise man, says Smith:

feels little pleasure from praise where he knows there is no praise-
worthiness, he often feels the highest in doing what he knows to be
praiseworthy, though he knows equally well that no praise is ever to
be bestowed upon it.[4]

Smith refers to the 'ingenious sophistry' of Mandeville.[5] And
accuses him of removing the distinction between virtue and vice in
a pernicious manner:[6]

---

[1] *Ibid.*, p. 225.

[2] *Ibid.*, pp. 487-88.

[3] *Ibid.*, pp. 488-89.

[4] *Ibid.*, p. 213.

[5] *Ibid.*, p. 493.

[6] *Ibid.*, p. 487.

There is an affinity between vanity and the love of true glory, as both these passions aim at acquiring esteem and approbation. But they are different in this, that the one is a just, reasonable, and equitable passion, while the other is unjust, absurd and ridiculous.[1]

According to Smith, vanity is the result of our selfish affections, whereas well-grounded reputation or glory results from the benevolent side of human nature. But, in any event, as Smith constantly repeated, conscience is the vital arbiter. We endeavour to examine our own conduct as we imagine any other 'fair and impartial spectator' would:[2]

When I endeavour to examine my own conduct, when I endeavour to pass sentence upon it, and either to approve or condemn it, it is evident that, in all such cases, I divide myself, as it were, into two persons; and that I, the examiner and judge, represent a different character from that of the other I.[3]

No man, said Smith:

during either the whole course of his life or that of any considerable part of it, ever trod steadily and uniformly in the paths of prudence, of justice, or of proper beneficence, whose conduct was not principally directed by a regard to the sentiments of the supposed impartial spectator, of the great inmate of the breast, the great judge and arbiter of conduct.[4]

Duty

Thus, Smith utterly rejects theories which blur or remove the distinction between virtue and vice. We may achieve much by pursuing our legitimate self-interest through mutual adjustment to

---

[1] *Ibid.*, p. 490.
[2] *Ibid.*, p. 204.
[3] *Ibid.*, p. 206.
[4] *Ibid.*, p. 422.

others, but any worthy human being should also seek to do right according to his sense of duty:

> That the sense of duty should be the sole principle of our conduct, is nowhere the precept of Christianity; but that it should be the ruling and the governing one, as philosophy, and as, indeed, common sense, directs.[1]

Such were the elevated principles which guided one of the founding fathers of classical liberalism, views which were shared with no less devotion by the later classical economists, from Ricardo, Senior and J.S. Mill to Alfred Marshall. During the twentieth century duty and conscience went out of fashion, especially after the Second World War and this has been reflected in modern classical-liberal writing. But Hayek has re-instated moral considerations to their central place in classical-liberal philosophy and we need to follow his lead in improving our own understanding of the moral conditions essential to a free society. Some American scholars, with Michael Novak in the lead, have already begun to take up this challenge.[2]

Summary

To sum up: the claim of collectivists that they are altruistic and that classical liberals favour selfishness is without foundation. Much of the talk of compassion and caring which typifies collectivist writing is, whether deliberately or unwittingly, disguised self-interest of the narrowest kind. Frequently it comes either from trade unions or 'professional' groups intent on cementing their own monopoly power or from egalitarians who seek to disguise their levelling doctrine behind a smoke screen of ostensible virtue. But a parade of compassion is not morality. Moral worth flows from the benefits of our actions for others, not the loudness of our demands for caring at someone else's expense.

---

[1] *Ibid.*, p. 269.

[2] See for example, Novak, M., *The Spirit of Democratic Capitalism*. New York: American Enterprise Institute/Simon & Schuster, 1982.

The false contention that to favour markets is to encourage selfishness is based on a confusion between self-interest and selfishness. Each of us has a legitimate and inevitable self-interest in the survival and welfare of ourselves and our families, which we pursue by mutual adjustment to others as we provide goods and services for them. It is, of course, possible for people to pursue their self-interest in a selfish manner, but no such attitude is approved or condoned by the classical liberals. They were unanimous in believing, not only that people should be induced by the checks and balances of the competitive marketplace to behave properly, but also that every person should seek to do right according to their conscience.

4

POSITIVE AND
NEGATIVE FREEDOM

Three concepts are central to the new collectivism: social justice, positive freedom and citizenship. This chapter discusses positive freedom, leaving the analysis of social justice and citizenship to Chapter 5. I will focus especially on the work of Professor Raymond Plant, one of the leading left-wing intellectuals attempting to rebuild collectivist thought. I will refer primarily to his most recent major work, *Conservative Capitalism in Britain and the United States*, written jointly with his American colleague, Kenneth Hoover.[1] As the deputy leader of the Labour Party, Roy Hattersley, recognises: 'No one in Britain has done more than Raymond Plant to rehabilitate the notion that to succeed, perhaps even to survive, the Labour Party needs to possess a theoretical framework within which to build its practical policies.'[2]

Plant and Hoover believe that the classical-liberal critique of social justice has dented left-wing orthodoxy and they set out to demonstrate the 'enduring relevance of the left's traditional concern with distributive issues'.[3] First, they defend the distinction between negative and positive freedom and fail to see the consequent danger of confusing freedom with power. Second, they defend egalitarianism against Hayek's criticism that 'social justice' is not justice at all. And third, they advocate citizenship, partly to offer the Labour Party a new basis on which to appeal to the

---

[1] Hoover, K. and Plant, R., *Conservative Capitalism in Britain and the United States: A Critical Appraisal.* London: Routledge, 1989.

[2] *Ibid.*, p. 319.

[3] *Ibid.*, p. 262.

32

electorate in place of social class, and partly because they contend that classical liberals in some way deny full rights of citizenship to part of the population.

Positive Freedom

One of the main targets is Hayek's conception of freedom, which Plant and Hoover call negative freedom. According to Plant and Hoover, advocates of negative freedom restrict 'citizenship' to civil and political rights and assign people no economic rights. Negative freedom, they say, does not 'entitle the citizen to any particular share of resources'. To assess this view we must first understand what Hayek says.

Clarity of Language

Hayek believes that distinguishing between positive freedom and negative freedom has given the false impression that there are two species of the same genus 'freedom'. But according to Hayek, negative freedom is concerned with individual autonomy whilst positive freedom means 'power' and forms part of a wider ideology which wants the power of the state to be used to bring about equality of outcome.

Freedom in the classical-liberal sense is negative in that it describes the absence of an evil, namely coercion by others. It does not assure us of opportunities, but as Hayek comments: 'while the uses of liberty are many, liberty is one'.[1] He goes on:

In the sense in which we use the term, the penniless vagabond who lives precariously by constant improvisation is indeed freer than the conscripted soldier with all his security and relative comfort. But if liberty may therefore not always seem preferable to other goods, it is a distinctive good that needs a distinctive name.[2]

---

[1] Hayek, F.A., *The Constitution of Liberty*. London: Routledge & Kegan Paul, 1960, p. 19.
[2] *Ibid.*, p. 18.

Hayek is not, therefore, engaging in an argument about the 'real' or 'correct' meaning of the term freedom, he merely wants to avoid equivocation in the use of terms, for if the same term means different things on different occasions there can be no rational debate and no progress towards truth.

Traditionally, advocates of freedom have been concerned with the scope and duties of government. The state plays a key part in preventing private acts of coercion by laying down a framework of rules which it will enforce against private force and fraud. These rules mainly stipulate what you may *not* do to others: kill, steal, break agreements, and so on. But, because it enjoys a monopoly of coercion, the government is also a potential menace to liberty which explains why classical liberals have been particularly concerned with the rights of the individual against the central power. The government, with the police, army and tax collectors at its disposal, can more severely impair individual liberty than any private organisation.

Hayek's goal is to understand that set of social arrangements which is most compatible with each individual functioning as an autonomous, thinking and valuing person. He defines 'coercion' as the opposite state of affairs:

> By 'coercion' we mean such control of the environment or circumstances of a person by another that, in order to avoid greater evil, he is forced to act not according to a coherent plan of his own but to serve the ends of another... Coercion is evil precisely because it thus eliminates an individual as a thinking and valuing person and makes him a bare tool in the achievement of the ends of another.[1]

Plainly a slave is not a thinking, valuing person but rather a mere tool of another's will. But coercion is a slippery concept and can easily be applied to any situation in which a person chooses the lesser evil, such as entering into an agreement with some degree of reluctance. If, for instance, I enjoy working in the open air but the only available job is as a farm labourer on relatively low pay,

---

[1] *Ibid.*, pp. 20-21.

am I coerced by the farmer? Egalitarians often speak of coercion as if it applied to all cases of reluctant acceptance of agreements and assume that each such instance justifies government intervention.

Why Restraint is Justified

But in deciding the circumstances in which government may legitimately promise to punish types of conduct it is important to remember why restraint is justified at all. It is in order to facilitate individual choice, not to attempt to remedy every dissatisfaction in civil society. This concern to limit the occasions on which governments may interfere coercively is sometimes confused with the view that any action in private life which does not harm others is permissible. Often called *laissez-faire*, this idea has been advocated by ultra-libertarians whose ultimate objective is no government at all and who believe that 'anything goes' in social life. For them all restraints, whether governmental or social, are bad. As Adam Ferguson, a contemporary of Adam Smith, warned:

> the vulgar conceive a zeal for liberty to consist in opposition to government...and seem to think that whatever impairs the power of the magistrate must enlarge the freedom of the people.

But, he contended:

> the establishment of a just and effectual government for the repression of crimes, is of all circumstances in civil society the most essential to freedom: That everyone is justly said to be free in proportion as the government under which he resides is sufficiently powerful to protect him, at the same time that it is sufficiently restrained and limited to prevent the abuse of its power.[1]

If some restraint of private activity by government is necessary, the central question is how best to apply restraint in order to

---

[1] Ferguson, A., *Principles of Moral and Political Science*, 2 vols., Hildesheim/New York: Georg Olms, 1975, vol. 2, pp. 458-9.

facilitate individual autonomy. In essence, classical liberals have argued that a 'rule of law' is preferable to the 'arbitrary rule of men'. That is, if there must be restraint then restraint through laws is more consistent with individual autonomy than arbitrary power, so that every person, as they go about their affairs, can take into account what the law prohibits or requires. Laws in this sense are warnings which enable us to avoid unwanted consequences if we so choose.

Hayek identifies four main requirements to which laws should conform. First, laws must be abstract, that is, they must not apply to specific persons, places or objects, but rather to types or kinds of persons, places or objects. This is intended to make it more difficult for law makers to grant special privileges to favoured factions or individuals. Second, they must be prospective and not retrospective so that individuals know where they stand. Third, the rules must be known and certain and therefore less open to perverse or self-serving application by judges. Fourth, they must apply to everyone equally and above all to the legislators as well as to others, in the hope of discouraging law makers from giving advantages to known groups, a practice which leads to the legislative process becoming a method of gaining advantages at the expense of others.[1] No less important than the *form* that state coercion takes is the *scope* of government. If every conceivable matter were dictated by law there would be little individual autonomy.

In spite of Hayek's careful argument that positive and negative freedom are not species of the same genus, but different things, Plant and Hoover interpret freedom as the capacity to act, that is they insist on using the term 'freedom' to describe 'power'. In doing so they appear to have misunderstood why Hayek values individual autonomy. Hayek's ideal is the thinking, valuing citizen and he contends that government restraint through a rule of law is necessary in order to grant people a sphere of action protected against pre-defined acts of coercion at the hands of others. This

---

[1] Hayek, *The Constitution of Liberty*, p. 209.

necessitates prescribing the impartial *form* that government action takes as well as limiting the *scope* of government. Individual autonomy in Hayek's sense is not advanced by calling on government to exert arbitrary power to equalize each person's material holdings because this would mean that everyone's life was open to unlimited manipulation by government. Thus, in the sort of society favoured by egalitarians a person might be able to prosper by hard work, investment or saving, but only up to that point approved by the government of the day. That is, people would be pawns in a game played by government. They would not be actors with their own values, thoughts and aspirations entitled to follow their own inclinations so long as they do not infringe pre-ordained laws designed to give everyone similar freedom.

Plant and Hoover call the tradition of freedom which emphasises the rights of the individual against the central power 'negative freedom', suggesting that it is inferior compared with positive freedom. Does the focus on checking state coercion make it any less attractive? We can understand this question better by comparing freedom with another negative concept 'peace'. Peace means the absence of war, but few would claim that *negative* peace is less desirable than *positive* peace.

If we follow Plant and Hoover's approach of applying the adjective 'positive' to peace, we can see more clearly the nature of their mistake. Imagine that 'negative' peace described a state of affairs in which there was no war and therefore greater opportunities to become prosperous. In this situation we can envisage that some people would work harder and longer than others and earn more money. And some would become wealthy through luck. How would we react if a political group began to demand 'positive' peace?—meaning that everyone should enjoy only the 'appropriate' share of the rewards they were able to reap because of the absence of war.

Most people would see instantly that peace—the absence of war—is a desirable and sufficient state of affairs in its own right and that advocates of 'positive peace' were applying an entirely separate principle, equalization. And they might note that the effect of calling this levelling doctrine 'positive peace' is to conceal its true character.

Useful Inequalities

A major difficulty with Plant and Hoover's approach is that they appear to assume a static start. They speak of *entering* markets and desire a fresh start but with a more equal distribution brought about by rectifying holdings at the starting-gate.[1] It is plainly true that there is a given distribution at any moment of observation but societies are dynamic entities. The distribution is changing constantly and we can never in practice start afresh. Everyone has a past history and the effort to rectify incomes and wealth at the conceptual starting-line may undermine something valuable in the arrangements which led to the distribution of holdings at the moment of observation. In economics this has usually been understood as undermining the incentive structure of differential rewards, an argument which Plant accepts within very narrow terms.

Like John Rawls before them, Raymond Plant and Kenneth Hoover desire to narrow material differences without impairing economic performance. They are contemptuous of equality of opportunity because, they say, not enough is done to eliminate background inequalities such as parental bequests.[2] Indeed, procedural equality of opportunity is described as disingenuous, because it is not equality at the starting-gate. They speak of the necessity for 'compression of the reward structure' and even of the desirability of restricting bequests to prevent parents from giving their children too much of an advantage.[3] It is also wrong, they say, to reward talent as 'prodigiously as we do'.[4] Note the use of the term 'we', which implicitly assumes some central apparatus deciding who deserves what.

---

[1] *Ibid.*, pp. 207, 212.

[2] *Ibid.*, p. 219.

[3] *Ibid.*, p. 220.

[4] *Ibid.*, p. 221.

38

While Plant and Hoover want to reduce the advantages that flow from talent for which the individual was not responsible, they are not absolute hard-line equalizers. They recognise that their approach restricts individual liberty and seek to develop a theory of 'legitimate inequality'.[1] They acknowledge two concerns: first, the adequacy of incentives and second, whether the process they call 'trickle down' helps the poor more than redistribution.[2]

Incentives

They accept with some reluctance that incentives are necessary for higher productivity and efficiency and describe the higher payment which is usually (but not always) made to people who have undergone training as a 'rent of ability'.[3] They express resentment towards people who are fortunate enough to be gifted and they particularly resent advantages due to family background, for which, they say, the individual deserves no credit. They see the 'rent of ability' as a pure economic criterion: it is that sum of money which will get a job done and without which society would be poorer. They say they do not want a pay board to fix such differentials but that there ought to be 'an onus to justify incentives'.[4] It is, however, very difficult to see how such a pervasive invigilation of pay could be operated without a central apparatus with some teeth.

Their hostility to differential rewards is flawed in two particular ways. First, they wrongly perceive the only justified differentials to be due to merit or desert in the form of effort expended on training, whereas there are other grounds. Second, their hostility to the family and their narrow focus on its contribution to enabling individuals to enhance their earnings ignores the vital role of the family in character building and moral training.

---

[1] *Loc. cit.*
[2] *Ibid.*, p. 223.
[3] *Ibid.*, p. 224.
[4] *Ibid.*, p. 225.

Low income may be the result of misfortune; it may also be the result of a failure to give good service. Redistributing incomes would fatally undermine the signalling mechanism by which we can tell whether or not we are contributing maximum service to our fellows. Moreover, if service to others does not determine income, other forces will do so. In Plant and Hoover's scheme, political power will determine individual earnings. In a classical-liberal society we cannot say that skill and hard work will always reap their reward, but we can say that an open society increases the chances of this being so and that it is desirable for that reason. Clearly if you are fortunate enough to have well-off parents who give you money, this confers an initial advantage over others who are less well placed. But performance counts and there are many examples of poorly-endowed people rising by their own efforts and of the well-endowed ceasing to be prosperous through incompetence or moral failure.

The Role of Competition

But the freedom of individuals to reap the reward of their own efforts is not the only issue. No less important is the role of competition in channelling individual efforts to the service of others. To the extent that income and wealth depend on providing goods and services for other people, competition ensures that only those who best satisfy the requirements of their fellows prosper. In Plant and Hoover's view, rewards should be 'compressed' which means that it will be less worthwhile troubling to give good service.

It can plausibly be claimed that material rewards at any given moment depend primarily on performance in meeting the requirements of fellow citizens. Luck counts, but to resent it and to desire coercively to eliminate its effects destroys opportunity and benefits no one. It may be that a company decides to sell a product because of a purely private passion of its owner, and that by sheer luck it proves successful. Nevertheless the company's action in selling the product remains meritorious in that it meets the requirements of others.[1]

It is of the utmost importance to recognise that rewards depend on the value of goods and services to the people who choose to buy them, not on the personal merits or needs of suppliers. For this reason Hayek regrets that market rewards have sometimes been justified exclusively as the deserved outcome of hard work or skill.[2] Individuals may justly feel proud of their success, but their pride should come from having given good service as judged by others. It is also permissible to be proud of hard work and skill but it should not be assumed that all success is due to personal qualities or effort. Success involves winning the voluntary support of fellow citizens, an altogether more humble basis for pride.

Trickle Down

Plant and Hoover recognise that is fruitless to aspire to equalize people if there is little or no wealth to redistribute. For this reason they seek economic growth, but their paramount concern remains equality. This focus on material equality enables them to see that material incentives are functional because they encourage people to exert themselves and thus to create economic growth. But it diverts their attention from a bigger reality, namely that it is the ethos of personal responsibility which is the real engine driving economic growth.

When speaking of the process whereby wealth is first created and then finds its way into the pockets of individuals and families, Plant and Hoover use the term 'trickle down', a notion which suggests a movement of money from the wealthy to the poor, and which conjures up an image of the poor receiving crumbs from the rich man's table. Is this an accurate way of thinking about the ideas articulated by the classical economists?

It is important to understand the nature of the societies the classical economists were hoping to escape from. The old medieval

---

[1] This is not to claim that all wants merit equal respect, only that there is no advantage in discriminating against good fortune.

[2] Hayek, F.A., *Law, Legislation and Liberty*. London: Routledge & Kegan Paul, 1976, vol. 2, p. 74.

order was hierarchical and static. Most people lived at subsistence level, year in year out, and from generation to generation. And most were born to a particular station in life. In rural areas there were few choices to be made: the village meeting in some localities or the lord of the manor in others, dictated which crops must be grown, when ploughing must begin, when to sow, which animals might be tended, and so on. In the towns, the guilds exercised detailed control over all aspects of work, including the products that could be made, the prices charged, the quantities produced and the methods, tools and materials that might be used.

During the seventeenth and eighteenth centuries it was possible to detect a radical change which was not fully articulated until the later part of the eighteenth century. Families, initially dotted here and there, later in large numbers, began to defy the old ways. They used their practical wisdom to improve the methods used to grow crops, rear animals and make useful goods for others to use. Dependent only on their courage and what today we might call their human capital, they defied the village authorities and tried new ways of farming, or they left for new localities where traditional authority was weak. Similarly, some families left the stifling atmosphere of the ancient boroughs for rural areas where the writ of the guilds did not run. Here they tried their hands at different methods of manufacture and trade. As it turned out, these pioneers prospered.

The lesson was that adherence to tradition in agriculture, animal husbandry and manufacturing created a static, hierarchical life at subsistence level for all but a few aristocrats. But, when individuals were set free to develop their own methods of farming and manufacture by trial-and-error, economic growth was the outcome. Prosperity began to spread as each began to share in the new wealth created by the application of human initiative and knowledge.

The essence of this revolutionary departure from the old order was free scope for human ingenuity and knowledge, which in turn assumes that individuals are taking personal responsibility for their own affairs, in religious and moral matters no less than in their work. The same families that took risks in growing crops in new ways or making products by different methods, also tended to prefer to elect their own preachers in a general meeting rather than to countenance the authority of bishops. And in hard times, they preferred the mutual aid of the church congregation or the friendly society to dependency on the parish.

Thus, the new prosperity which enabled the vast majority to escape from the old, unchanging, social order was the result of individuals who were willing to take risks by applying their own practical knowledge in their work. Consider now the attitude of modern egalitarians. They show no awareness of the centrality of personal responsibility, human ingenuity and human capital in generating prosperity. The egalitarian's eyes are focused on relative rewards and whether they are deserved. If talent gives rise to a higher income, they are concerned to impose a penalty, particularly if the talent is natural or has been encouraged by attentive parents. They have not understood that personal responsibility is still the determining factor. There are many naturally talented individuals who have squandered their endowments and it is not unknown for the children of the wealthy to live frivolous, futile lives.

Classical liberalism puts personal responsibility at the centre; the focus of the egalitarian on material relativities is simply too narrow. But there is another aspect of 'trickle down' which egalitarians neglect. Democratic capitalism has in practice produced greater material equality compared with the old order which it replaced. And if we compare all the inequalities of Britain, not only with pre-capitalist history, but also with modern communist countries then we find that wealth in Britain is *more*, not less, equally distributed. Communist countries have declared equality to be their goal for decades, but the reality has been very different and the price in lost liberty very high. Eastern-European experience should deter us from allowing the state to become too powerful in pursuit of apparently benign objectives. Should we take the same risks in order to 'compress' income differences or reduce the ratio between the poorest and the richest person? So long as the standard of life of the poorest person is acceptable, why should the state be concerned at all with income relativities?

43

Egalitarian Materialism

Nor do Plant and Hoover reveal any awareness of the relative triviality of the egalitarian ideal. Hayek's inspiration is a free society in which individuals, in mutual concert with their fellows, can conceive and pursue their own version of the good life, thus enabling unknown persons to contribute to the good of others by innovation or achievement in industry, services, the arts and voluntary work. The ideal is to maximise the chances for everyone to live a full life in all its dimensions. In contrast, the egalitarian's focus is narrow and material. Perhaps without being fully aware of it, egalitarians appear to see people merely as consumers, or satisfaction seekers, and desire only to equalize their power to consume material goods, and then only up to the point at which economic growth would be impaired. It is true that earlier egalitarians like Tawney and Titmuss argued that greater material equality would raise the non-material aspirations and pursuits of the poor. And it is plainly true that someone who is hungry will be pre-occupied with finding their next meal at the expense of more elevated concerns. But this is an argument for protecting people from material hardship. It does not follow that we must all be equal in material possessions, or even more equal than we are now, in order to live a culturally richer life. Once people have risen above subsistence level the richness of their culture is an independent variable. History offers many examples of wealthy people who have lived shallow and even debauched lives and no fewer examples of people with little to call their own who have enjoyed a more elevated existence.

Civil society is far more than an economic reward system. In particular, families are essential institutions for raising responsible citizens by moral training and developing character. Parents have a natural desire for their children to succeed but to the egalitarian, the family is primarily a source of 'unfair' advantages. The giving of such advantages by parents is resented and egalitarians urge that they be removed, cancelled or 'compressed'. If they achieved their aim they would undermine one of the main forces for good in the world, the powerful natural desire of parents to help their children do well. How much harm has the pursuit of equality already done

44

to the family? And if such measures do undermine the family, has this weakened it as a character-building institution vital to civic harmony? No such question occurs to the egalitarian.

Egalitarianism Corrupts Democracy

No less important, egalitarians have failed to see the dangers of extending state power. Their focus on positive freedom derives from their desire to bring about equality of outcome and Plant and Hoover's comment that Hayek concedes a connection between freedom and power suggests that they may not have understood Hayek's underlying concern. Plant and Hoover argue that Hayek concedes some connection between freedom and 'abilities' (i.e. power) when in *The Constitution of Liberty*[1] he accepts that a monopoly supplier of water in a desert may coerce people. Hayek objects to monopoly because the monopolist can strip people of the opportunity to function as responsible, choosing agents. And he values liberty because he anticipates that some people will put it to good use, to the ultimate benefit of all. But Hayek stresses that we do not know in advance who will be the innovators and that we must, therefore, ensure opportunities for all.

The essential point is that Hayek is concerned with the *life chances* of *unknown* persons. Plant and Hoover's focus is on the present material condition of *known* groups of individuals such as the lowest earners at a given moment. They appear to see no real danger in licensing party politicians to bid at elections for support by offering to confer additional income on large sections of the population at the expense of others. Above all, they do not see that democracy is thus transformed into a vote-buying process in which every person must be concerned to enhance or at least protect his material position against intrusion by others armed with the powers of the state. Hayek's goal is to avoid this corruption of democracy by confining government as far as possible to the role of rule maker and enforcer. Experience of private law enforcement

---

[1] Hayek, *The Constitution of Liberty*, p. 136; Hoover and Plant, *Conservative Capitalism in Britain and the United States*, p. 209.

should have warned us of the necessity to fight for an impartial state. Private policing led historically to blood feuds and excessive vengeance because people are apt to attach too much importance to their own concerns. And just as people tend to over-punish transgressors when their own immediate interests are affected, so people are too fond of their own comforts to be trusted to use state power to redistribute the incomes of others.

Redistributive 'justice' is undesirable because it provides a basis for discretionary political power. Traditionally classical liberals contended that government must enjoy a monopoly of coercion so that individuals know they can only be coerced by one agency and this agency must coerce through general laws which each person can take into account in advance. Individuals know that any conduct not prohibited is permitted and are thus free to develop their own talents. This is in the interests of all because we never know in advance who will make a worthwhile contribution. The market enables us to discover the unknown and unpredictable. Compare this with a society based on 'social justice'. Individuals would be able to go about their own affairs but no one would be permitted to make more than an approved multiple of the lowest income. This would put limits on capital accumulation and prospects for innovation. Or, if there was no declared ratio, but only a commitment to 'compression' as Plant and Hoover propose, then we would face arbitrary political power because the government would be entitled to 'rectify' any material outcome it did not like.

I suggested in Chapter 1 that egalitarians' dislike of inequality is partly aesthetic. Adam Smith described the desire to make everyone conform to a pattern as a 'love of system':[1]

The man of system...is apt to be very wise in his own conceit, and is often so enamoured with the supposed beauty of his own ideal plan of government, that he cannot suffer the smallest deviation from any part of it. ...he seems to imagine that he can arrange the different members of a great society with as much ease as the hand arranges

[1] Smith, A., *The Theory of Moral Sentiments*. Indianapolis: Liberty Classics, 1969, p. 305.

46

the different pieces upon a chess-board; he does not consider that the pieces upon the chess-board have no other principle of motion besides that which the hand impresses upon them; but that, in the great chess-board of human society, every single piece has a principle of motion of its own, altogether different from that which the legislature might choose to impress upon it.[1]

Plant and Hoover show some awareness of the danger that the state's power may expand too far but they generally prefer to think of demands on the government as 'culturally defined' rather than politically defined.[2] For instance, they accept that 'needs' are politicized and tend to grow, and therefore that some constraints make sense.[3] Accordingly, they concede that there is no obligation on government to provide for all self-defined 'needs' if the similar demands of others are put at risk. They also agree with Rawls that there is no duty to equalize if total resources would be reduced.[4] In defence of their far-reaching proposals, they point out that the limited safety net of classical liberals is also open to political pressure. This is true, but it is plainly less open to political pressure than the extensive government intervention they envisage.

It is important to distinguish between the relief of hardship and equalization. The former is consistent with limited government whilst the latter provides a rationale for unlimited arbitrary power. It is true that the accepted view of what constitutes hardship will change with general prosperity but if the minimum standard of living is defined at a particular time in terms of a basket of goods, then this sets a clear limit on the Government's power.[5] The basket of goods, can change over time as the consensus on the accepted minimum changes and to avoid constant political pressure for change or adjustment the basket of goods might be fixed for a 5 or 10-year period. By contrast, both the desire to bring people

1 *Ibid.*, pp. 380-81.
2 Hoover and Plant, *op. cit.*, p. 211.
3 *Ibid.*, p. 217.
4 *Ibid.*, p. 218.
5 For a discussion of public perceptions of necessity see Mack, J. and Lansley, S., *Poor Britain.* London: Allen & Unwin, 1985, esp. p. 53 *et seq.*

up to the constantly-changing average wage and the vague ambition to compress income differentials allow wide scope for state coercion.

Market Forces and Political Forces

Plant and Hoover complain that the market will 'dominate' more and more of our lives.[1] In their scheme, however, political power is to dominate. They do not see the qualitative difference between market forces and political forces. Classical-liberal or market principles describe a *process* in which people are free to pursue their own version of the good life. In the social order desired by egalitarians most spheres are to be politicized, with the result that the government will predominate in dictating what the good life shall be. Nor do egalitarians seem conscious that the poorest people are at a disadvantage in a highly politicized system. In a free society those poor people who hope for a better life can fulfil their aspiration by a purely personal choice to work hard and save from their earnings. An egalitarian society requires the ambitious poor to organise politically to fulfil their hopes.

Plant and Hoover are very concerned about economic concentration, which, they believe, has implications for political power. Economic power, they say, cannot be dismissed from the political agenda because money can buy political power. Yet, they are not so concerned about political power as such.[2] Free marketeers, they say, are naive about the impact of economic power on politics.[3] On the contrary, classical liberals are suspicious of all concentrations of power, private or public, and urge competition and the maximum room for individual initiative in order to encourage the wide dispersal of economic power. Egalitarians display no awareness that power concentrated in political hands is a far more menacing threat than power in private hands. Imagine that one of the leading car manufacturers somehow established an absolute

---

[1] *Ibid.*, p. 231.

[2] *Ibid.*, p. 228.

[3] *Ibid.*, p. 229.

monopoly on car production. They would have a massive income but the worst thing any such company could do would be to push up car prices or perhaps make bad quality and unsafe cars. This would be thoroughly undesirable, and in a competitive market competitors would soon replace them, but consider what is the worst action a government could take? It has the police, prisons, tax collectors and the army, enabling it to kill, torture, imprison, confiscate possessions and take away individual rights.

The egalitarian might retort that a monopolistic company might have so much money it could buy political power. This may be so but then the threat would be from the abuse of *political* power not economic power. We would have come full circle. The fundamental problem remains how to avoid the abuse of state power. The remedy is to put severe limits on the uses of political power so that no amount of economic power can buy unlimited political power. And just to be on the safe side, one of the tasks of government should be to enforce competition to discourage concentrations of economic power and promote wide dispersal of resources. It does not matter how many cans of Coca-Cola or motor cars or anything else a company sells, the money it accumulates does not become a threat until it is transformed into political power. The power to direct the police, the army, the prisons and to levy taxes are the means to take away individual liberty and, therefore, the primary abuses to be avoided.

No less important, market competition disperses power by allowing people to accumulate capital. This makes it more difficult for governments to become over-mighty by concentrating all power in their own hands. Far from threatening individual liberty, economic freedom is the indispensable means of protecting it.

Idealism and Naivety

The lack of awareness of the dangers inherent in extending state power stems from assumptions about human nature and behaviour. Put at its simplest, some egalitarians are motivated by hatred and some by love, and those motivated by love tend to be sanguine about how good people will speedily become. Over the years socialists have won a good deal of support because of their optimistic view of human nature. But the credit they have won is largely misplaced because it rests on a confusion between, on the one hand, the factual belief that people will quickly become good citizens, and on the other, a private determination to live the life of a good citizen by aiming personally to achieve the highest possible standards of conduct. Individuals who strive to become good and upright citizens deserve the highest praise; individuals who believe that the majority will very quickly come to achieve human perfection are naive. More seriously, if they propose to remodel national institutions on the assumption that the majority will always be good and upright in all their dealings, they are a menace.

Classical liberals assume that people are corruptible. To some this is regrettable because it suggests that classical liberals do not believe it worthwhile to strive for perfection. But to recognise the truth of a state of affairs is not to accept or condone it, nor is it to dismiss efforts aimed at improvement. As the work of Adam Smith amply testifies, ethically classical liberals call for people to act according to conscience and to strive for the highest standards. But simultaneously classical liberalism faces the truth that people are corruptible and seeks to take appropriate precautions. In politics, therefore, classical liberalism calls for checks and balances to prevent the abuse of government power. And in economics, competition is advocated to deter selfish conduct. Socialists, however, make insufficient allowance for human fallibility. The classical liberal is no less enthusiastic about aiming for the highest standards of human conduct, but urges only that we do not create institutions which assume that man has already been perfected or can be perfected. The practical result of making this latter assumption has everywhere been rapid disillusion, leading to a search for scapegoats, followed in quick succession by persecution of all opponents.

Egalitarians do not seem to have understood that they have erected a theory which justifies arbitrary power and that in their favoured world people would be unable to be certain in what respects they remain free to act and in what respects unfree. The practical importance of such uncertainty for the confidence essential to long-term investment is vividly demonstrated by the plight of Hong Kong in the shadow of the Chinese takeover.

More than Negative Freedom

Classical liberalism is not concerned only with the rights of the individual against the state, so-called negative freedom. The term negative freedom does not accurately sum up the classical-liberal view of the role of government, which is that government has an indispensable role in maintaining and enforcing rules prescribing just or right conduct between individuals and other persons. It is only because such power can be abused that classical liberalism is also concerned with limiting government power. The ultimate goal is not the total absence of government, but that balance between individual and government most compatible with the independent, thinking, valuing person.

Thus, we may make three distinctions. First, there are the rules governing private relations, enforced by government. Second, there are rules putting limits on what government may do in order to prevent abuse of its own power. Third, as Adam Smith clearly saw, there are the private relationships themselves, which are guided by moral principles not backed by the threat of official punishment but by private expressions of approval or disapproval. Classical liberalism is parodied as being about negative freedom, when manifestly it is about far more than that. The term negative freedom refers only to the limits on government advocated by classical liberals, not the enforceable rules of justice which underpin liberty, nor the moral order on which freedom also rests.

5

SOCIAL JUSTICE
AND CITIZENSHIP

Plain Justice or Social Justice

Hayek believes that three factors have been undermining personal freedom in the West. First, the lack of awareness of the limits of human knowledge and the corresponding tendency to over-estimate the ability of governments to plan the affairs of the nation. Second, the idea that political freedom must entail unlimited popular sovereignty, which in reality means unlimited government. And third, the demand for social or redistributive justice on which this paper focuses. According to Hayek, 'social justice' has produced a willingness to use the coercive apparatus of the state, not to see fair play between citizens according to established rules, but to adjust the material positions of particular groups in accordance with the government's preferences.

Hayek counsels against the abuse of the term 'justice', which historically described the idea of fair play according to established and impartial rules, that is, rules which took no account of persons. According to Hayek, this original concept of justice is barely understood in the West today, and increasingly commentators speak not of justice but *social* justice. They have in mind, not personal conduct as judged against a moral or legal standard, but some concrete state of affairs like the rate of pay of a given set of employees or the share of national income of some segment of the population. It is considered unjust that the rich should enjoy so much wealth and unjust that the poorest section of the population should receive only a certain proportion of the nation's income.

52

Hayek's criticism is that, strictly speaking, only human conduct can be called just or unjust:

If we apply the terms to a state of affairs, they have meaning only in so far as we hold someone responsible for bringing it about or allowing it to come about. A bare fact, or state of affairs which nobody can change, may be good or bad, but not just or unjust.[1]

No one would think of calling natural occurrences like bad weather or earthquakes either just or unjust.

The Clear Use of Language

Once more Hayek is insisting on the clear use of language. To some this insistence may seem to be pointless or purely 'semantic'. It is possible to engage in fruitless disputation about the meaning of words and thus fail to get to the heart of the matter, but Hayek's complaint is different. Not to be concerned to use language clearly, he says, is to be unconcerned with truth, either when it is stated in simple propositions or when inferred by valid reasoning. Equivocation is probably the most widely practised logical error and the telescoping of distinctions is currently a common type of equivocation in political theory. Justice strikes most people as a good thing and political philosophers naturally try to present their preferences in language that adds to their appeal, but the desire to present a case in attractive terms should not override the obligation to reason validly without ambiguity. 'Justice', in the sense of conforming to impartial rules, is different from 'social justice', in the sense of using the power of the state to equalize material possessions. The language of political discourse should make the difference clear because to telescope such distinctions is to engage in propaganda not scholarship.

Hayek's judgement on political philosophers who abuse language is severe, but he acknowledges that the great majority of people who use the term social justice believe it is no more than an

---

[1] Hayek, F.A., *Law, Legislation and Liberty*. London: Routledge & Kegan Paul, 1976, vol. 2, p. 31.

innocent expression of goodwill towards the less fortunate. Hayek contends that it is no such thing. Ultimately social justice is:

> based throughout on the atrocious idea that political power ought to determine the material position of the different individuals or groups—an idea defended by the false assertion that this must always be so and socialism merely wishes to transfer this power from the privileged to the most numerous class.[1]

Since the shares of national income people end up with are neither intended nor foreseen he claims that the term 'justice' should not be applied to them. In its proper use the term justice means infringing some pre-established rule requiring or prohibiting specified conduct. A mere state of affairs can infringe no such rule.

However, Hayek does not believe that each nation-state must always automatically accept any and every given distribution. He acknowledges that past injustice can be rectified but holds that unless such injustice is clear and recent it will generally be impracticable to correct it.[2] For example, a wealthy British family which inherited land originally bestowed on a distant relative by William the Conqueror should be left alone, but there might be a case for the redistribution of huge estates in some Latin American countries where land was seized by force from native indians earlier this century.

Nor should Hayek's view be confused with opposition to all measures to assist the poor. He criticises the concept of social justice because, by putting each person's material position at the disposal of the government and focusing on the relative position of groups, it provides a basis for the corruption of the democratic process. He regards a safety net for those unable to fend for themselves as essential.

Nor is he wholly opposed to any effort to appraise the overall fairness of a given social order. He urges only that in assessing its fairness or desirability we put aside our awareness of our own

---

[1] *Ibid.*, p. 99.
[2] *Ibid.*, p. 131.

54

material position in it. His alternative method of appraising the 'fairness' or attractiveness of a whole society or culture has much in common with Rawls' technique of deciding on the desirability of a social order from behind a 'veil of ignorance', that is without knowing what our own position in it would be.[1] Essentially Hayek believes that laws should increase the life chances of *unknown* persons:

> All the law can do is to add to the number of favourable possibilities likely to arise for some unknown person and thus to build up an increasing likelihood that favourable opportunities will come anyone's way.[2]

We should, therefore, regard as the most desirable order of society:

> one which we would choose if we know that our initial position in it would be decided purely by chance (such as the fact of our being born into a particular family).

Put another way, 'the best society would be that in which we would prefer to place our children if we knew that their position in it would be determined by lot'. In these circumstances very few people, he believes, would choose either an egalitarian order in which the government sought to level each person down to some official standard or one in which riches were available to the few, as we find in aristocratic societies. Instead, most would choose an industrial society which offered the great majority the opportunity to thrive by their own efforts, and provided an acceptable minimum for the less fortunate.[3] For instance, if you had a chance to live in the eighteenth century and you knew you would be an aristocrat you might find the idea attractive, but if your position in the eighteenth century was to be assigned randomly, the chances

---

[1] Rawls, J., *A Theory of Justice*. Oxford: Oxford University Press, 1973.

[2] Hayek, F.A., *Law, Legislation and Liberty*. p. 130.

[3] *Ibid.*, p. 132.

are you would be a peasant or a servant. A society in which each individual's lifestyle is a matter for personal choice and which offers the prospect, but not the guarantee, of success for all those who are willing to work, is far more attractive.

Confusing Justice and Benevolence

Professor Plant criticises Hayek's contention that the total distribution of income and wealth is neither intended nor foreseeable by anyone and, therefore, not a matter of justice in the traditional sense of the term. In *Conservative Capitalism*, Plant and Hoover appear to accept that the overall pattern of material holdings is not intended by anyone, any more than the weather is intended, but they believe that this misses the point that for some groups some results are foreseeable. More specifically, Plant and Hoover claim that, 'as a general rule, those who enter a market with least will end up with least'.[1] Thus, poverty is a foreseeable result of starting with a small share, even if the outcome was not intended by any other individual.

As I have already argued, the claim that we can foresee that poverty will lead to further poverty is over-stated. Having money is a help, but it is no guarantee of success. A person can start with nothing and through effort, skill and diligent service, become very prosperous. Indeed, the chief difficulty for the low-paid worker who wishes to advance by hard work and saving is the high rate of income tax on low incomes which has resulted from pursuing policies of equalization since the Second World War.

In any event, the important question for Plant is not how market outcomes have been *caused*, but how we *respond* to them. He believes that our reactions to misfortunes, such as poverty, can be just or unjust. He contends that the just response is to accept collective responsibility for redistributing resources at the starting-gate because only in this manner can we avoid the poverty which is the foreseeable result of the initial maldistribution.[2]

---

[1] Hoover and Plant, *Conservative Capitalism in Britain and the United States*, p. 207.

[2] *Ibid.*, p. 212.

56

In response to my claim in *The New Right*[1] that the presence of hardship requires *action* but not necessarily *government* action, Plant and Hoover say that the rectification of injustice is not a matter of private charity any more than the infringement of property rights is a private matter.[2] First, it can be objected that charity is not the only private alternative. Self-help within the family and neighbourhood has always been important, but of no less significance has been mutual aid. For instance, some 9 million out of the 12 million covered by the 1911 National Insurance Act, one of the earliest of the measures inaugurating the welfare state, were already providing themselves with benefits equal to or better than those supplied under national insurance. They did so through the friendly societies, those private, voluntary collective agencies for mutual aid whose members eschewed dependence on others and prided themselves on their self-reliance.[3]

Second, Plant fails to acknowledge the difference between means and ends. Real hardship should indeed be relieved but we should not rule out the possibility of employing methods other than government programmes. There are several reasons for considering private alternatives, as J.S. Mill understood. Government ventures which entail compulsion to the extent that they are financed from taxation, but in no other respect, are not automatically ruled out by Mill so long as the government does not establish a monopoly, and so long as it leaves people free to pursue similar aims. However, Mill still identifies some powerful objections. There is an objection if a service could be carried out more effectively by private agencies; and even when the government might carry out a function more effectively than private individuals, it might still be better to provide it privately as a method of educating people in citizenship, that is, making available opportunities to improve their active, intellectual and moral qualities. No less important, the more tasks a government undertakes the more likely it is to do them

[1] Green, D.G., *The New Right: the Counter-Revolution in Political, Economic and Social Thought*. Brighton: Wheatsheaf, 1987, pp. 127-29.

[2] Hoover and Plant, *op. cit.*, p. 216.

[3] Green, D.G., *Working Class Patients and the Medical Establishment*. Aldershot: Temple Smith/Gower, 1985.

badly. Similarly, Mill warns that the government's power should not be too great because each addition 'causes its influence over hopes and fears to be more widely diffused';[1] and, above all, if democracy is not to drift into totalitarianism, people must be able to gain the experience necessary to direct practical affairs independently of government.

The third defect is that the presence of hardship is qualitatively different from infringing property rights. Professor Plant appears to assume that any good thing can properly be achieved by coercive state action. But there is a distinction between justice and benevolence as Adam Smith understood the term. Justice refers to the limited occasions when the government is entitled to punish individuals for harming others. Benevolence means the *un*limited opportunities available to us for doing good. If our possessions are stolen we are harmed and the government can punish the culprit. Such intervention can be kept within limits, but if government is entitled to use its powers of coercion to remedy income differences—for instance, because a person earns less than average earnings or falls within the lowest quintile—then there is no limit to how such powers might be applied.

Thus, Plant and Hoover's argument confuses justice—the enforcement of rights through laws formulated to reduce the risk of abuse of government power—with benevolence, which, because it is potentially without limit, can never be a basis for government intervention without providing a justification for unrestricted power. Benevolence, as Adam Smith clearly saw, is vital to a decent society but it should be primarily (though not exclusively) a matter of private duty, not political agitation.

Citizenship

Citizenship theory owes its recent origins to T.H. Marshall and Richard Titmuss. Marshall's view of history was that by the twentieth century people had gained civil and political rights and

---

[1] Mill, J.S., *On Liberty*. Everyman edn. London: Dent, 1972, p. 165.

that the purpose of the welfare state was to supply additional social rights without which people could not be full citizens.

Titmuss disliked markets intensely and hoped to see market values entirely replaced by welfare values, a view which still has support among some social policy analysts. But the bulk of the new citizenship theorists do not share this desire completely to replace markets. They want the prosperity delivered by market competition, but believe that market relations need to be supplemented. David Harris, one of the more authoritative citizenship theorists, shows that this was also the approach preferred by T.H. Marshall:

> I am one of those who believe that it is hardly possible to maintain democratic freedom in a society which does not contain a large area of economic freedom and that the incentives provided by and expressed in competitive markets make a contribution to efficiency and to progress in the production and distribution of wealth which cannot, in a large and complex society, be derived from any other source.[1]

The main complaint about markets is the lack of altruism. According to Harris, market relations are 'coldly calculating' and characterised by 'mutual indifference'. Moreover, by 'legitimating the competitive pursuit of self-interest a society encourages not merely indifference towards others but selfishness and acquisitiveness'.[2] Yet, despite these doubts, Harris declares that he prefers Marshall's awareness of the importance of private economic markets to Titmuss' 'emotional hostility'. He does not, therefore, aspire to eradicate the market altogether, only to 'constrain its operation and compensate for its failures'.

Notwithstanding the fundamental differences over the role of markets, citizenship theorists are agreed that the purpose of the welfare state is to integrate people into the community. Welfare

---

[1] Quoted in Harris, D., *Justifying State Welfare: The New Right Versus the Old Left*. Oxford: Blackwell, 1987, p. 65.

[2] *Ibid.*, p. 62.

benefits, therefore, are not considered to be public charity. They are an entitlement which must be given universally as of right to (a) avoid stigma, (b) compensate victims for misfortune, and (c) enable people to achieve the consumption standard necessary to play their part as full citizens. Means testing, whilst not wholly rejected, is to be avoided because it marginalises the poor. Professor Ruth Lister, for example, insists that we need to be reminded of our mutual inter-dependence and urges that the welfare state should not merely provide a safety net. Under a welfare state which provides only for the poor, the beneficiaries will be considered failures, she claims.[1] Benefits for the poor, runs the old catch-phrase of Titmuss, 'will become poor benefits' because the poor become isolated or 'marginalised' so that the rest of the population no longer has a real stake in defending them.[2]

Citizenship's Electoral Appeal

To these traditional arguments Professor Plant has added a new party-political reason for citizenship. In a Fabian Society pamphlet[3] he explains why it is necessary to identify for the Labour Party a new basis on which it can appeal to the electorate. In essence, he argues that there are not enough manual workers for an appeal to social class to succeed. Until recently the Labour Party has tried to combine its traditional working-class support with an appeal to interest groups like homosexuals and inner-city black activists, but this has also failed to win elections. Plant argues that Labour, therefore, needs a new rallying cry and he recommends 'citizenship'. Labour's citizenship is also contrasted with the narrow view of the citizen which leftists attempt to associate with free marketeers, namely that man is a consumer and no more.

The weakness of citizenship theory is that its adherents have not understood that universalism intensifies the corruption of vote-buying and middle-class subsidies. Nor have they a clear view about

---

[1] Lister, R., 'Conclusion II: There is an alternative', in Walker and Walker (eds.), 1987, p. 141.

[2] Ibid., p. 142.

[3] Plant, R., Citizenship, Rights and Socialism. Fabian Tract 531. London: Fabian society, 1988.

60

the purpose of welfare to compare with the classical-liberal view that its objective is to provide temporary relief in the hope of restoring independence. The policies of the CPAG and like-minded lobbies trap people into reliance on state benefits. Nor is there the slightest reason to suppose that benefits would inevitably be reduced to 'poor benefits' if confined to people in hardship.

Moreover, where is the concern for social solidarity in telling people they can enjoy many benefits at the general expense? Far from generating one nation, this breeds division and antagonism and turns the political process into a battleground for consumption at the expense of other people. Titmuss intensely disliked private altruism which he dismissed as involving a 'gratitude imperative'[1] but he did not see the emergence of a political 'gratitude imperative' built on buying votes with promises of spending at the general expense. But even without the vote-buying, welfare benefits do not necessarily integrate people. Indeed, this is acknowledged by David Harris, one of the more discerning of the citizenship theorists. He claims that welfare benefits may have the opposite effect of generating conflict in the sense of a scramble for benefits and cites John Goldthorpe, a sociologist, who points out that some rights have promoted social conflict by increasing the bargaining power of organised labour.[2]

Perhaps the most telling criticism of the new citizenship theorists is that their concept of welfare rights is based on a very narrow conception of where the rights come from. Advocates of welfare rights talk much of compassion, caring and social justice, but the emphasis has been placed on the individual's claims on the public purse. Contrary to the assertions of its adherents, it is based on a narrow view of people as consumers, takers, or satisfaction seekers, not as givers or contributors to the common welfare. In reality, their view ironically takes its conception of human nature from the narrowest sort of selfish individualism, emphasising access to

---

[1] Quoted in Harris, *op. cit.*, p. 59.

[2] *Ibid.*, pp. 78-79.

'patterns of consumption'. According to David Harris, for instance, if someone lacks the means to enjoy the:

social benefits and consumption opportunities which are generally available, then he is excluded from his society's way of life and has a *prima facie* claim on the resources required for him to secure readmittance.[1]

It is a one-sided doctrine containing no notion of reciprocity or where the 'welfare rights' come from. And not withstanding the frequent rhetoric about participating in the community, it does not respect people as functioning actors in their own right but rather sees them primarily as passive recipients of gratuities.

The alternative classical-liberal view accepts that in a civilised society we should without hesitation help people in hardship; but it is also concerned that everyone who can contribute to the common good should do so. This means that when anyone temporarily cannot contribute, the objective of social policy should be to identify the source of failure and seek to restore independent self-reliance as quickly as possible. Social policy in recent years, with its emphasis on sending cheques through the post, has not achieved this aim. Instead, it tends to trap people in a dependent condition in which they become incapable of contributing as free citizens to the good of all, including themselves.

Today, the concept of citizenship is being offered as a new basis for national solidarity, implying simultaneously that classical liberals have no commitment to citizenship. But on the contrary, we are now seeing a contest between two competing visions of citizenship: on the one hand the *equalized* citizen and on the other, the *morally-responsible* citizen. Under the former view, the 'good life' is determined by politicians in the political process; whereas under the latter, the role of the state is to facilitate the freedom of individuals to choose the 'good life' for themselves in mutual but voluntary association with their fellows.

[1] *Ibid*, p. 148.

To sum up: the end-product of the new egalitarianism is a re-labelling of equality. Most people think justice is a good thing and so equality is described as a kind of justice, namely social justice. Most people also believe that freedom is a good thing and so equality is said to be a kind of freedom, namely positive freedom. Citizenship is also a word which offends few and attracts many and so equality is also said to be citizenship. Full citizenship, it is argued, should entail not only *civil* rights but also *social* rights. But all the talk of social justice, positive freedom, citizenship and social rights cannot conceal the fact that equality is what is desired and that equality is the name for the political theory which justifies the power of the state being used to equalize people.

6

CONCLUSION

I have argued that social justice retains its grip on public opinion for four main reasons. The first is that the relief of hardship is confused with equalization. The result is to provide an excuse for unlimited and arbitrary political power. The second reason is that egalitarians foster the political belief that voters can profit at the expense of others. This transforms politics into a vote-buying process. Third, equality is said to create social solidarity or 'one nation'. Social solidarity is a good thing but it can be secured without equalizing people by making available opportunities with the added protection of a safety net. Equality is not essential to solidarity. The fourth factor explaining why social justice retains its sway is that advocates of equalization claim to repudiate self-interest and to embrace altruism. The reality is that equalization has nothing to do with altruism; indeed, it often promotes selfishness.

Most people who express support for social justice feel they are doing no more than declaring their good intentions towards the poor. And to call for positive freedom in addition to mere negative freedom seems no less laudable. But such thinking is profoundly misguided. Support for social justice is not an innocent expression of goodwill towards those who are down on their luck; it is a demand which in the end undermines the personal freedom of all. This reality has been concealed in part by the confusion of language in political debate. Nothing but obfuscation can come from talking about separate ideas as if they were the same or similar, as we do when we speak of positive and negative freedom as if they were types of freedom and when 'social justice' is considered a type of 'justice'.

Classical-liberal principles are said to foster selfishness, but on the contrary, the central concern of the classical-liberal tradition has been to discover that set of social arrangements, public and private, which best enables people with different goals, thoughts, values and aspirations to live together with the minimum conflict. It is centrally concerned with discovering the best way to curb selfishness without creating a monster in the form of a state machine which threatens liberty more than private human selfishness.

The plausibility of the egalitarian claim that classical liberals encourage selfishness is based on the confusion of selfishness with self-interest. We all have an inevitable and legitimate self-interest in our own survival and that of our families, but we can pursue that self-interest selfishly or unselfishly. The contention that markets condone or encourage selfishness is without foundation, as the writings of the classical economists amply testify. On the contrary, market competition tends to channel potentially selfish energies into the service of others.

Despite the ugly reality of full-blooded socialism on the experience of every nation which has attempted to enforce it, socialist proclamations of altruism and their optimism about human behaviour seem at first sight to reflect well on them as idealists who aspire to a high ideal of perfection in human conduct. By comparison, classical liberalism does not come over as an ideal at all. It is seen as being essentially about facing the economic facts of life. This is partly because the era of Thatcherism has been dominated by reversing Britain's economic decline, but also because the main carriers of classical-liberal thought in recent decades have been economists who have been concerned with economic efficiency. To that extent they have departed from the wider concerns of the founding fathers of political economy. The uncompleted task of classical liberals is to combine the pragmatism of capitalist economics—which seeks to check greed through competition and to avoid tyranny by creating dispersed power—and the realism of capitalist politics—which aims to limit political abuse and corruption by means of democratic checks and balances—with a new voluntary capitalist moral order which fosters personal moral responsibility and seeks to promote benevolence without politicizing every walk of life.

Other Health and Welfare Unit Publications

Competing for the Disabled

September 1989, £5.00. ISBN 0-255 36256-0

PROFESSOR C. S. B. GALASKO, *Consultant Orthopaedic Surgeon, Manchester*
PROFESSOR IAN McCOLL, *Director of Surgery, Guys Hospital*
CAROLINE LIPKIN, *IEA Health Unit*

'It would be wrong to this IEA publication as simply another broad right-wing sideswipe at state-funded health provision. It offers a level of detail and thoughtfulness which is likely to appeal beyond its normal constituency.' *Health Service Journal*

If you need a wheelchair you are advised to be rich . . . Governments should not, [the authors] conclude, both finance and control the production of health care services, since the disadvantages are borne by the disabled.' *The Lancet*

Perestroika in the Universities

November 1989, £5.00. ISBN 0-255 36257-9

PROFESSOR ELIE KEDOURIE, *London School of Economics*

'The Government was yesterday accused of seeking to "nationalise" the universities by increasing central control over their activities through the new Universities Funding Council. Professor Kedourie said it was "quite mysterious" that a Conservative administration should follow a university policy "so much at variance with its proclaimed ideals".' *The Times*

Medical Care: Is it a Consumer Good?

April 1990, £3.95. ISBN 0-255 36258-7

BRENDAN DEVLIN, *Consultant Surgeon, North Tees General Hospital*
IAIN HANHAM, *Consultant Radiotherapist and Oncologist, Westminster Hospital*
JAMES LE FANU, *General Practitioner*
ROBERT LEFEVER, *General Practitioner*
BRIAN MANTELL, *Consultant in Radiotherapy and Oncology, The London Hospital*
MICHAEL FREEMAN, *Consultant Orthopaedic Surgeon, The London Hospital*

'Devlin . . . points out that the quality of practice is by no means assured: doctors, he claims, do not always elicit the correct history, and they can overlook or misinterpret physical signs; 30-40% of appendices removed in Britain show no evidence of appendicitis.' *The Lancet*